Symmetry i[n the World]

by Sarah Feldman

Table of Contents

What Is Symmetry?

This beautiful building is called the Taj Mahal. It is in India and was completed in 1643. Imagine that you could draw a line right down the middle of the Taj Mahal, from top to bottom. What would you notice?

Maybe you would notice that both halves of the Taj Mahal are exactly alike. Each side is a **mirror image** of the other.

That means that the Taj Mahal has **symmetry**. We say something has symmetry when both halves match exactly.

The Taj Mahal has perfect symmetry.

It's simple to see symmetry in shapes. If you have a circle, and you fold it in half, both sides will be the same shape and size. Both sides will match. That means a circle has symmetry.

If you have a sheet of paper shaped like a square, and you fold it in half, both halves will look the same. That means a square has symmetry.

Another way to say a shape has symmetry is to say the shape is **symmetrical**.

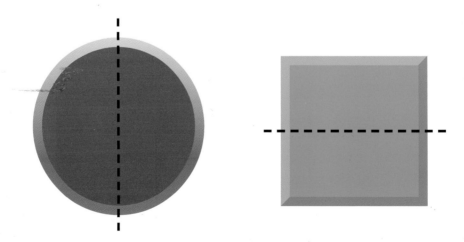

The circle and the square are symmetrical.

Which Flags Have Symmetry?

Look at these flags.
Which ones are symmetrical?

What about other kinds of shapes? Take a pencil or crayon and draw a curvy shape, like a big fluffy cloud. It might look something like the one you see on this page.

Now imagine cutting out the shape you drew and folding it in half. Would the two halves match exactly? Probably not.

The shape you made most likely does not have two sides that match. The shape you drew probably does not have symmetry.

Shapes that do not have symmetry are called **asymmetrical**. Asymmetrical means "without symmetry."

Draw a curvy shape.
Is this shape symmetrical?
Let's find out.

Does a Triangle Have Symmetry?

Shapes like squares and circles are always symmetrical. Their two halves always match. Some triangles have symmetry. But some triangles do not.

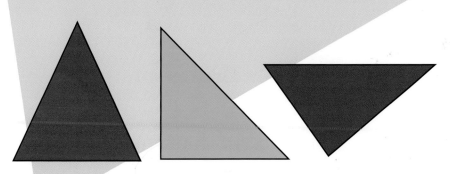

Which of these triangles is symmetrical?

Fold your shape in half. If the two halves do not match, your shape is asymmetrical.

Can You Find **Symmetry** in the Alphabet?

Some alphabet letters are symmetrical, and some are not. Can you figure out which letters have symmetry?

Let's look at the uppercase letters of the alphabet. We'll start with **H**. If you divided the shape of the letter **H** in half, is the right side the same as the left? Yes, both sides are mirror images of each other. **H** is a symmetrical letter.

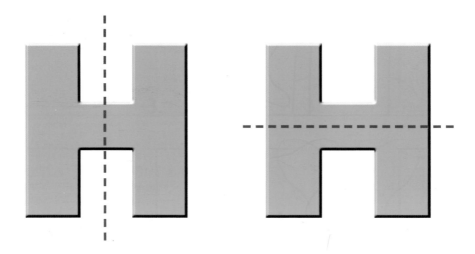

What about **F**? No, if you "fold" the letter **F** in half, both sides would not be the same.

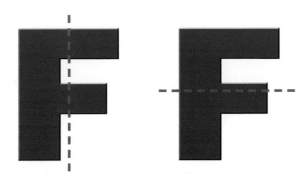

How about **B**? That's tricky. If you fold or divide **B** in half one way, it is symmetrical. If you fold or divide **B** in half the other way, it is not symmetrical.

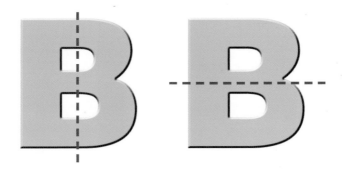

Try to see which other letters are symmetrical, which are asymmetrical, and which of the letters in the alphabet are sometimes symmetrical.

Do You Have Symmetry?

Does the human body have symmetry? If you look at your body on the outside, it seems so. Your face is nearly symmetrical with two eyes and two eyebrows. But do your eyes match exactly? Your ears?

Inside your body, your brain is symmetrical. It is divided into two even parts called lobes. You have two lungs and two kidneys—one on each side of your spine.

But you have only one heart and one stomach. So maybe you are not really symmetrical.

What do you think?

Are you symmetrical?

Make a Symmetrical Shape

Here's an easy way to make a symmetrical shape:

1. Fold a sheet of paper in half.

2. Get a pencil. Draw a shape—any kind of shape or blob you want—along the fold, using the fold as one side or part of your shape.

3. With the paper folded over, neatly cut out your shape.

4. When you're done, you'll see that you've cut out a perfectly symmetrical shape!

What Is the Line of Symmetry?

Remember the imaginary line you drew down the center of the Taj Mahal?

Look at the fold in the paper shape you just made. It makes a line down the center.

In the middle of every shape with symmetry is a line, real or imaginary, that divides it into two equal halves. This is called the **line of symmetry.**

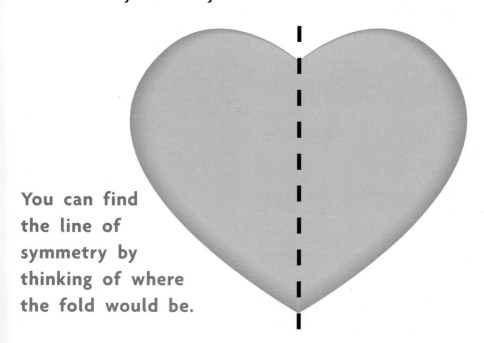

You can find the line of symmetry by thinking of where the fold would be.

Can You Find Symmetry in Nature?

Now that you know how to look for it, you'll see that symmetry is everywhere. Nature is full of examples of symmetry.

Butterflies have symmetry. Both halves of a butterfly match. One wing is the mirror image of the other.

The middle of the butterfly's body makes its line of symmetry.

Do you see symmetry in the butterfly?

On the beach, the sand dollar has symmetry. Farther down the beach, you might spot a symmetrical scallop shell. That same beach might have a clam or crab with symmetry, too.

Sand dollars, snowflakes, crabs, and scallops have symmetry.

In the forest, you'll find many leaves with symmetry. In a deep, dark, asymmetrical cave, you may find a symmetrical bat (if you're brave enough to go inside in the first place)!

Deep in the jungle, you might come face-to-face with the symmetrical stripes of a tiger.

You can't fold a pineapple in half. But if you had a picture of a pineapple and folded it in half, you would see that pineapples are symmetrical.

Where else do you find symmetry?

Even pineapple slices are symmetrical.

Glossary

asymmetrical (AY-sih-MEH-trih-kul): without symmetry; a shape that does not have two equal halves

line of symmetry (LINE UV SIH-meh-tree): a line that divides a symmetrical shape into two equal halves

mirror image (MEER-er IH-mij): the same arrangement of an item or pattern, but reversed, as though it were reflected in a mirror

symmetrical (sih-MEH-trih-kul): having symmetry, or two equal halves

symmetry (SIH-meh-tree): having two equal halves that match exactly

Index